Buddhism

Your Personal Guide to Healing Your Life, Achieving Happiness and Finding Inner Peace

By Maya Faro

Copyright Maya Faro©2016

Maya Faro© Copyright 2016 - All rights reserved.

Legal Notice:

This book is copyright protected. It for personal use only.

Disclaimer Notice:

Please note the information contained in this document is for educational and entertainment purposes only. Every attempt has been made to provide accurate, up to date and completely reliable information. No warranties of any kind are expressed or implied.

Readers acknowledge that the author is not engaging in the rendering of legal, financial, medical or professional advice. By reading this document, the reader agrees that under no circumstances are we responsible for any losses, direct or indirect, which are incurred as a result of the use of information contained within this document, including, but not limited to, errors, omissions, or inaccuracies.

The following are quotes from prominent Buddhist teachers:

"No one saves us but ourselves. No one can and no one may. We ourselves must walk the path."

-The Buddha

"Letting go gives us freedom, and freedom is the only condition for happiness. If, in our heart, we still cling to anything - anger, anxiety, or possessions - we cannot be free."

-Thich Nhat Hanh, *The Heart of the Buddha's Teaching: Transforming Suffering into Peace, Joy, and Liberation*

"If we learn to open our hearts, anyone, including the people who drive us crazy, can be our teacher."

-Pema Chödrön

"If there is any religion that could respond to the needs of modern science, it would be Buddhism."

-Albert Einstein

"The secret of Buddhism is to remove all ideas, all concepts, in order for the truth to have a chance to penetrate, to reveal itself."

-Thich Nhat Hanh, *Buddha Mind, Buddha Body: Walking Toward Enlightenment*

"It is my conviction that there is no way to peace - peace is the way."

- Thich Nhat Hanh, *The Art of Power*

"A great human revolution in just a single individual will help achieve a change in the destiny of a nation and, further, can even enable a change in the destiny of all humankind."

- Daisaku Ikeda, *The Human Revolution*

"Whether our action is wholesome or unwholesome depends on whether that action or deed arises from a disciplined or undisciplined state of mind. It is felt that a disciplined mind leads to happiness and an undisciplined mind leads to suffering, and in fact it is said that *bringing about discipline within one's mind is the essence of the Buddha's teaching.*"

- Dalai Lama XIV, *The Art of Happiness*

Contents

Introduction 13
What is Buddhism 15
A brief history of Buddhism 17
Buddhism in today's world 20
The Source of all problems: 22
Self-Identification with the mind 22
You are the source of your reality 28
Lifting the veil of the mind's illusions 31
    Exercises for strengthening your concentration 32
    Exercise 1 32
    Exercise 2 34
    Exercise 3 40
    Exercise 4 42
    Exercise 5 43
    Exercise 6 45
More on Buddhist philosophy 49
The Four Noble Truths 51
    Exercise 7 54
The Buddhist perspective of God 58
    Exercise 8 59
Living the Buddhist Teaching 61
    Bonus Chapter: The Skills of Mindfulness 62
    When You Feel Happy 64
    When You Feel Anxiety 64
Final Thoughts 70

Introduction

There was a servant who had worked for years serving his master at his beckon call. The master lived in a large mansion but would never leave his room. Whenever he wanted his servant, he would call the servant, who would come to the door of the master's room. The door was always locked, so the servant would listen to his master's orders through the closed door. One day, the servant was performing his duties when he saw a maid who also worked at the mansion. The servant shared with the maid how he was becoming more and more displeased with his master. "I have worked for my master for many years, and I do everything he asks me to do, yet he is never pleased. Nothing is ever good enough for him; he always wants more and more." The maid told the servant that he should talk to the master about this and let him know how he felt. The servant thought about what the maid said. He had realized that he had always listened to the master without ever questioning him. He was so frustrated at this point that he decided that he would talk to the master.

The servant went to the master's door and called his name but there was not response. He then knocked on the door, still no response. The master then turned the door knob and the door opened slightly. The servant could not believe it; the door was unlocked. Never before had the door not been locked! The servant gathered his courage and entered his master's room; what he saw left him stunned. His master's room was completely empty; there was no furniture, no master! The servant stood in the empty room in despair, realizing that he had spent all these years serving someone who did not exist.

The story of the servant and his master represents the essential teaching of Buddhism, which is to become master of our minds, instead of our minds becoming to master of us. Just like the locked room that contained an illusionary master, our minds are constantly issuing thoughts to us, which we frequently observe without questioning.

There are various schools of Buddhism, which may vary in their practices; however, they all share a common focus, to transcend the mind so as to provide greater mental clarity, greater happiness, greater compassion, and greater freedom in our daily lives. This book not only explores Buddhism and its philosophy, it offers exercises that provide the reader with an opportunity to make practical application of this ancient wisdom.

What is Buddhism

There was a young man who wanted to learn about Buddhism. He knew of a wise monk, who lived in the nearby hills, so he went out to find him. After hiking for a few hours, the boy saw the monk sitting by a stream. The boy asked the monk "What is the purpose for practicing Buddhism?" Without saying a word, the monk took a clear glass jar and filled it with water from the stream. He then scooped up some sand from the bottom of the stream and poured it into the jar as well. The monk gestured to the boy to follow him as he made his way back to his hut.

Inside the hut was a small table and chairs. The monk told the boy to sit down and then proceeded to shake the jar and placed it on the table. The sunlight from the window shined on the jar; however, its rays became scattered as they passed through the jar. The suspended sand in the water caused its rays to break up as they passed through the murky water. The monk offered the boy some lunch and, when they were finished, the monk pointed to the jar. While they were eating, the sand had settled to the bottom of the jar, and the water was crystal clear. This time, the sun's rays passed through the jar without any hindrances. The monk said to the boy, "The jar represents your mind. The sand represents your thoughts, and the water is your awareness. The jar with the murky water is the undisciplined mind. The jar with the clear water represents a disciplined mind. That is the purpose of practicing Buddhism.

Anyone can learn to trade their endless parade of thoughts for the crystal clear waters of awareness without adopting a new belief system or faith. Buddhism is about having the direct experience of the most fundamental aspect of your being, which cannot be described in words. It is hoped by this book that you will be inspired to begin the transformation from murky water to clear.

A brief history of Buddhism

Around 2000 years ago, a young prince named Gautama would have a spiritual experience that would lead to one of the world's major religions as well as blurring the lines between religion and modern day science. For most of his childhood, Gautama's experience of the world was the interior of his father's palace. His father did not want Gautama to experience the harsh realities that existed on the streets of India. His father wanted Gautama to take over his kingdom when he became older.

Around the time that he reached his late teens, Gautama made the decision that he would leave the palace and explore the world outside the palace walls. What he saw left a powerful impression on him. He saw people who were sick, people who were old and feeble, and he saw the corpses of those who had died. Gautama had experienced the suffering of others. Gautama decided to make it his mission in life to find a way to relieve people from suffering.

In the following years, Gautama studied under many teachers, most of whom were of the ascetic tradition. The life of luxury that he was born to was replaced by self-imposed hardship on his body and mind. He starved himself, exposed his naked body to India's harsh elements, lived outdoors in the wilderness, and engaged in activities that further abused his body. He mastered all the teachings that he was taught, yet he remained unsatisfied; he was no closer to understanding how to rid others of suffering. The hardships of the teachings that he had practice hand not made him enlightened.

One day, Gautama decided to abandon all his teachers and rely solely on himself to find his answer. He found a quiet spot by a river, under a Bodi tree, and began to meditate. He made the determination that he would remain silent and still for as long as it took to understand the nature of suffering. Until then, he would not move from his place under the Bodi tree. During his meditation, he encountered many thoughts and images that were created by his mind, all of which threatened to distract Gautama from his meditation and break the commitment that he had made with himself. In the end, Gautama won the battle with his mind; he transcended it and became enlightened. It was then Gautama would be called the "Buddha" or awakened one.

Gautama would spend the remaining days of his life teaching others of what he discovered. When he died, his teachings were recorded in writing by his disciples. Known as sutras, these writings would make their way from India to China, Japan, and other parts of Asia, where different lineages developed. Though the foundations of his teachings would remain, each lineage developed its own practice for achieving enlightenment.

Buddhism in today's world

We live in a time that is unprecedented in human history. Our standard of living today would be considered science fiction or fantasy fifty years ago. We have 24 hour media cycles, high speed internet, quantum physics, GPS, and other technologies that offer us greater opportunity for enhancing our lives as never before. Despite all these advances, the level of our collective happiness, fulfillment, and wisdom has not kept pace. For all our advances, we have not invested the same kind of determination to understand the nature of who we are. We are like the murky water in the jar that is preventing our innate wisdom from shining through. This wisdom, known as the Buddha nature, is being eclipsed by our undisciplined mind. We live out our lives with and endless parade of thoughts passing through our consciousness, many of which preoccupy our attention. The purpose of Buddhism is to transcend our thoughts by disciplining our mind.

Think about your own life. What is happening in your life that is preventing you from experiencing inner peace or equanimity? What is preventing you from experiencing true happiness, a happiness that is independent of other people, situations, or events? We so often believe that happiness or inner peace is contingent upon us getting some kind of result in our lives. That result we are looking for maybe a healed relationship, or freedom from an existing relationship. The result that we are looking for may be overcoming our thoughts of the past or the forgiveness of ourselves or others. Perhaps what we are looking for is overcoming financial hardship or physical illness.

Regardless of what we are looking for, it will not lead to true happiness. If we fail to achieve the result that we are looking for, we will either become disenchanted, disappointed, or continue to strive to achieve that which we are looking for. If we achieve the result that we worked for, we may enjoy the feeling of happiness and success, but it will only be temporary. With time, our sense of victory will diminish, and we will start pursuing a new desire, or a new challenge will appear in our lives and steal our attention from our victory.

The Source of all problems:
Self-Identification with the mind

There is nothing wrong with desire or our pursuit of it; desire is both natural and necessary. Nor is wrong to feel disappointed for not achieving what we want or victorious for achieving our dream. In fact, our thoughts and emotions have nothing to do with happiness or unhappiness. Our thoughts and emotions are just part of life; they are forms of energy that we experience. The difference between feeling successful or a failure in life has nothing to do with the thoughts and emotions that we experience; rather, it is our relationship that we have with them that makes a difference.

When we identify with our thoughts and emotions as being an aspect of who we are, then our sense of self will constantly fluctuate with the changes in the thoughts and emotions that we experience. When we are experiencing positive thoughts, we may say to ourselves or others "I am feeling good." If we experience a setback or concern, we may say to ourselves "I am worried" or "I failed." In fact, any thought or word that follows "I" can become an aspect of our identity if we believe it.

Do the following exercise by reflecting on what you say to yourself, or to others about yourself, on a regular basis. Here are some examples:

- "I am a good person."
- "Nobody ever gives me a chance."
- "I am inpatient."
- "I am an angry person."
- "I will always be poor."
- "I am lucky."
- "I am a winner."
- "I am a loser."
- "No one loves me."
- "I am love."

Make a list of the thoughts or emotions that you most often experience. These thoughts or emotions have an affect on your sense of self. Whether they are positive thoughts or negative, what we say to ourselves and the emotions we feel, on a regular basis, will become part of our identity. The challenge is that if our experience in life does not remain consistent with our sense of identity, our sense of well-being will become threatened.

Think about the last time your sense of well-being was unstable. What were the situations or events that elicited this feeling? When you have identified the situation or event, go back to your list and review the items that you wrote. Did the situation or event conflict any of the items on your list? Now think of the last time you had a sense of well-being. What were the situations or events that resulted in this feeling? Going back to your list, was the situation or event consistent with any of the items on your list?

A person who is angry walks into a room where there is a dog. The dog responds to the person by keeping its distance. If there are people in the room, they may keep their distance as well. The resulting actions of those in the room will in turn have an effect on how the person experiences the situation. The person may be indifferent to the dog and feel undesirable that others people are not engaging him in conversation.

On another occasion, this same person walks into the room feeling peaceful. The dog approaches him, wanting to be petted. This brings about a sense of affection from the person. People in the room start engaging this person in conversation, and soon he may be part of a group that is enjoying a good time. The person now feels accepted and connected with those around him.

With either scenario, the outcome of this person's experience had nothing to do with the room, the people in it, or the dog. In fact, it had nothing to do with feeling undesirable or peacefulness. What made the difference was how this person experienced himself. In the first scenario, the person experienced himself as an indifferent and undesirable person, while in the second scenario; the person experienced himself as an affectionate or peaceful person.

From a Buddhist perspective, it is irrelevant what this person was feeling or experiencing. What is relevant is that this person was identifying with his mind. The person was telling themselves, at some level of their being, "I am an undesirable person" and "I am a peaceful person." From the Buddhist point of view, this same person would be thinking "The feeling of being undesirable is arising" and "The feeling of peacefulness is arising." Buddhism teaches us that we are not our thoughts, emotions, or other mental functions; rather, we are the witness of these mental functions as they arise within us. In order to demonstrate this, do this exercise:

1. Sit or lie down and close your eyes. Allow yourself to relax.
2. Enhance your relaxation by placing your attention on the flow of your breath. Breathing normally, place your attention on the flow of your breath as you inhale, and the flow of your breath as it leaves your body during exhalation.

3. As you relax further and your mind becomes clearer, visualize a beautiful sunset. Visualize it with as much detail as possible. Note: Everyone visualizes, though this ability varies from person to person. Some people are able to see their visualizations in vivid detail, while the visualizations of others can be very vague or faint. This does not matter. Just make your visualization as real as possible according to your ability.
4. Now visualize a black cat, see it as vividly as possible.
5. Lastly, visualize a full moon. Again, make it as real as possible.
6. Now open your eyes.

During this visualization exercise, you visualized a beautiful sunset, a black cat, and a full moon. At no time did you confuse yourself for any of these visualizations. You knew that you were not the sunset, the black cat, or the full moon; you were the observer of these things. These visualizations were just thoughts that took on a visual dimension. Unlike the person in the proceeding scenario, you did not identify with these thoughts. The reason for this is that these thoughts were not considered as being important by your mind, so there was no self-identification with them. On the other hand, the person in the room scenario placed importance on his thoughts. Because of this, he took on the qualities of his thoughts; he became indifferent, undesirable, affectionate, and peacefulness.

This same exercise can be modified by using emotions instead of thoughts; however, we will explore this in a later chapter as people have greater difficulty discerning the difference between themselves and their emotions than with thoughts.

You are the source of your reality

If we are not our thoughts or emotions, than who are we? What is the nature of the self? Buddhism believes that our true nature is that which is non-changing and eternal.

Imagine a house of mirrors as seen in carnivals and circuses. Upon stepping into the house of mirrors, you find reflections of yourself throughout the room. You know intellectually that what you are experiencing is the numerous reflections of yourself created by the walls of mirrors that make up the room. Upon leaving the house of mirrors, you find yourself in what you experience as the "real world," where numerous people, objects, and landscapes surround you. All of these things are seen as being other than you. There is never confusion that what you experience in your daily life is something that is separate from you. This kind of perspective is what most of humanity experience in their daily lives. In Buddhist philosophy, the house of mirrors is the accurate representation of reality. What we commonly refer to as the world, our environment, or our surroundings, is really a mirror reflecting our inner world.

We can never know true reality as everything that we experience is a projection of our own minds. To illustrate this, let us use snakes as an example. When you see a snake (or anything for that matter), information or data about the snake is taken in by your eyes. This information is then broken down by the optic nerve, which turns the information or data into electrical impulses. When these electrical impulses reach the brain, it converts the electrical impulses into an image. This image is enhanced by the information received by the other senses (touch, sound, smell, and taste), which are processed in the same way as sight, though through their respective sensory organs. Linguistically, we apply the label of "snake" to this image, based on the language that we know.

Not only do we assign a name to this image, we also assign meaning to it, which is based on our past experience or past learning. All of these processes work together to create our experience of "snake." Since everyone processes information differently, that which is called "snake" creates a different experience for each person. For most people, "snake" means something that you avoid, fear, or find distasteful. For others, "snake" is a source of fascination, admiration, and even affection; it all depends on how the information is processed.

Regardless of how we experience our mental representation of "snake," we never experience the ultimate reality of a snake. Everything that we experience is a projection of our own minds. We are not in the world; the world is within us. Even that which you refer to as "you," is just another projection of your mind. What is commonly referred to as "I" or "me" is a thought of which you have a very strong sense of identification with and have cultivated since the day you were born. The common spiritual adage "We are spiritual beings having a human experience" is completely accurate.

When you can understand what has been stated in this paragraph on an experiential level, not intellectually, your experience of yourself, others, and the world will take on a dramatic shift. You will go through life with a sense of equanimity, wisdom, compassion, and happiness that is most rare. Because all things in life are connected, your state of life will affect other people in a manner that supports their happiness as well as yours. This is the fundamental reason for the existence of Buddhism, to relieve suffering and create happiness in this world. To practice Buddhism means to be a scientist of your own being. It means to become quiet and still for the purpose of observing the mental functions of your mind so that you can take charge of it, rather than allow your mind to be in charge of you. One of the most powerful tools for this is contemplative practices that include concentration and meditative techniques.

Lifting the veil of the mind's illusions

All of our challenges in life, without exception, are relational. In other words, a problem cannot exist in isolation; it can only exist if we have a personal identification with it. If we hear of a person of whom we do not know, who is experiencing life threating injuries, we would not consider it a challenge for us. If the person with life threatening injuries happens to be us or someone we love, then we will most likely feel challenged by it. From the perspective of deeper levels of consciousness, the person with life threatening injuries, the life threatening injuries, and our own sense of identity are nothing more than a forms of thought.

The reason why we love deep sleep is because we are free of all challenges or sense of identity. In deep sleep, awareness is free from thought, so there is no experience of it. In deep sleep, we lose all sense of self, of identity, or sense of experience. This is evidence that the truth of who we are is not thought; it is awareness. By practicing contemplative exercise that strengthen our concentration and expand our awareness, we can have a direct experience that will transform our sense of who we are as well as our experience of life.

Exercises for both concentration and meditation are important if we are to understand the true nature of existence, which is consciousness. Exercises for strengthening our concentration are needed in order that we can discern our thoughts, emotions, and sensations so that we can observe them. Meditation exercises are needed so we can relinquish our need to control our minds so that we can discover the essential nature of our own being. When we become skillful in both of these practices, we can enjoy a new found freedom as all our problems and the questions that we have about ourselves and our lives will gradually fade away. At the same time, you will find yourself happier and more effective in your daily life. The reason for this is that we will lose our sense of identification with our thoughts, and our sense of identity becomes increasingly established in what is referred to as our Buddha nature, or pure consciousness.

Exercises for strengthening your concentration

Exercise 1

The purpose of this first exercise is to experience a purer kind observing by reducing the impact of your mental concepts.

Anytime we employ our minds while experiencing life, we add our own interpretations to our experience. Do the following:

1. Sit down and make yourself comfortable.
2. Take a few minutes to scan your environment, observing the people, plants, animals, or objects that are within your vicinity.
3. Now close your eyes and imagine that you are from another planet and have been sent to planet Earth to gather information about it. Being that you are from outer space, you have no previous knowledge or experience of Earth. You are like a newborn baby seeing the world for the first time.
4. Now open your eyes and look around again as you did the first time, remembering not to interpret, label, or judge anything that you see. Observe as though you were a blank slate.

How did your second observation compare with your first one? Many people report that their second observation seemed fresh and more vibrant, that they felt more connected to life and themselves, that they felt more peaceful. If you were unable to detect a difference between the two observations, continue to practice until you are able to discern a difference.

The value of this exercise is that it provides the cultivation of nonjudgement and perceiving without coloring it with your own personal interpretation.

Exercise 2

The purpose of this exercise is to challenge your sense of relationship with your environment. We were raised believing that who we are is a separate entity from that which we are experiencing. In other words, when I look at my dog, I see him as being a separate being or object that exist outside myself.

Note: You will be asking yourself a number of questions when performing this exercise. Answer the questions based solely on your direct experience at that moment, not what you know intellectually.

1. Sit down and allow yourself to relax.
2. Breathing naturally, place your attention on the flow of your breath as you inhale and exhale, noticing the sensations that you experience.
3. When you feel relaxed, select an object for observing.

4. Observe the object for a few seconds, allowing your eyes to be relaxed, do not strain them.
5. As you observe the object, determine whether the act of seeing is separate from the object or not. In other words, does seeing stop at a certain point, at which the object begins, or does the act of seeing and the object merge into each other as one?
6. Now determine if the act of seeing begins from within you or does it occur from the outside of the body.
7. Next, ask yourself if you are aware of seeing? In other words, how do you know that you are seeing? Note: The question is regarding the process of seeing, not that which is being seen. How do you know the process of seeing is occurring? Are you aware that "seeing" is taking place? As indicated before, do not think of the correct answer to this question; only go by your direct experience at this moment.
8. Confirm for yourself that seeing and the object being seen are not separate, that they indeed flow into each other as one.
9. Confirm for yourself that seeing occurs from within the body, not outside of it.
10. Confirm for yourself that there is the awareness of seeing, that at some level of your being, there is a knowing that seeing is taking place.

If you can confirm all of these points, we are left with the following conclusions:

1. The process of seeing and the object being seen are inseparable; they are one.
2. Seeing originates from within you. From this, we can logically conclude that both the process of seeing and the object being seen are found within you as well.
3. There must be awareness that seeing is taking place; otherwise, how would we now that seeing is occurring?
4. The process of seeing and the object that is being seen occurs within awareness.
5. You are aware of your existence.
6. You, the process of seeing, and the object being seen are inseparable; they are all one in the same.
7. You are awareness itself.

This exercise may seem esoteric or philosophical but do not be fooled. If you can directly experience these conclusions for yourself, you will be light years away from most of humanity, which believes that they are a separate object. All problems arise from seeing ourselves as being separate. As long as we see ourselves as being separate from those around us, we will always experience limitation, lack, frustration, or the need to persuade others to see our point of view.

The previous exercise can be repeated with the remaining sensory modalities as well:

Sensation or touch:

1. Close your eyes and touch an object.
2. Confirm for yourself that the sensations of the object being touched and the object itself are not separate, that they indeed flow into each other as one.
3. Confirm for yourself that sensation arises from within the body, not outside of it.
4. Confirm for yourself that there is the awareness of sensation, that at some level of your being, there is a knowing that sensation is taking place.

5. If you can confirm all of these points, we are left with the following conclusions:
6. When touching (with closed eyes) we cannot distinguish between the sensation and the object being touched.
7. Sensation originates from within you. From this, we can logically conclude that both the process of touching and the object being touched are found within you as well.
8. There must be awareness that sensation is taking place; otherwise, how would we now that sensation is occurring?

9. The sensation of the object and the object being touched occurs within awareness.
10. You are aware of your existence.
11. You, sensation, and the object being touched are inseparable; they are one in the same.
12. You are awareness itself.

Hearing

1. Confirm for yourself that hearing and the sound being heard are not separate, that they indeed flow into each other as one.
2. Confirm for yourself that hearing occurs from within the body, not outside of it.
3. Confirm for yourself that there is the awareness of hearing, that at some level of your being, there is a knowing that hearing is taking place.

If you can confirm all of these points, we are left with the following conclusions:

1. The process of hearing and the sound being herd are inseparable; they are one.

2. Hearing originates from within you. From this, we can logically conclude that both the process of hearing and the sound being heard are found within you as well.
3. There must be awareness that hearing is taking place; otherwise, how would we now that hearing is occurring?
4. The process of hearing and the sound being heard occurs within awareness.
5. You are aware of your existence.
6. You, the process of hearing, and the sound being heard are inseparable; they are all one in the same.
7. You are awareness itself.

This exercise can be applied to the sensory modalities of smell and taste as well but will not be elaborated on.

The previous exercises were selected to start the process of challenging your perception of reality by focusing on the aspects of experience that you are already familiar with: sensory and the awareness of it. If you were able to experience the indivisible relationship between sensory perception, the objective being perceived, and yourself, you have taken the first step in freeing yourself from the illusions that are created by the mind. If you had trouble with these exercises, I recommend that you continue you practicing them. With the next exercises, you will be focusing on your inner world.

Exercise 3

1. Sit down and make yourself comfortable.
2. Close your eyes and allow yourself to relax.
3. Place your attention on your breath as it enters and exits your body, focusing on the sensations you experience as you inhale and exhale.
4. The objective of his exercise is to keep your attention focused on your breath.
5. Inevitably, your focus will be distracted by your thoughts. Whenever you find your mind wandering, gently redirect your attention to your breath.
6. Do not judge yourself or any of your experiences, to do so will empower your mind. Regardless of how often you allow your attention to roam, just redirect your attention to your breath.
7. As you improve your ability to focus on your breath, you will experience a reduction in your thoughts and a greater sense of peace. Do not be surprised if your mind becomes restless after entering this calm period; it is normal. Just return your attention to your breath and your sense of calm will return and become more lasting.

This exercise has two benefits: The strengthening of your concentration and the realization that you have the power to gain control over your thoughts.

Now that you have had the experience of regulating your thoughts, you will now increase your awareness to the nature of emotions. Our thoughts and emotions are two different manifestation of life's energy, and they mirror each other. Everything that exists is made of energy and this energy manifest as phenomena, including thoughts and emotions. Our emotions are the physical manifestation of thought; they allow us to understand the nature of the thoughts that we are experiencing via the sensations of the body.

The quality of our emotions indicates the quality of our thoughts. If you are experiencing the emotions of anger, it is because you are having angry thoughts. If you change your thoughts, you change your emotions. If you change your emotions, you change your thoughts. Most of us try to avoid experiencing our emotions, particularly the negative ones.

The purpose of the next exercise is to demonstrate to yourself that no thought or emotion can have power over you unless you allow it. Our thoughts and emotions are dependent upon us for their power; they lack any power of their own. All of their power is borrowed from the attention that you give them.

Exercise 4

1. Sit down and make yourself comfortable.
2. Close your eyes and allow yourself to relax.
3. Place your attention on your breath as it enters and exits your body, focusing on the sensations you experience as you inhale and exhale.
4. Identify any negative emotions that you may be experiencing. If you are not experiencing a negative emotion, think of a problem or negative past experience. When you experience a negative emotion, offer it total acceptance. Do not try to avoid it, deny it, or change it; allow the emotion to fully express itself.
5. Place your full awareness on the emotion, allow yourself to observe it with your attention but do not engage it. Allow yourself to experience the sensations that accompany the emotion. Pretend that you are diving into the emotion; allow yourself to become fully immersed in it. Remember, your emotions have no power as long as you do not try to resist them to or try to interpret them. As long as you involvement with them is restricted to observing them and experiencing them, you will be in charge.
6. What happens to the potency of your emotions when you just observe them and allow them to fully express themselves?

Exercise 5

This next exercise will involve you playing a more active role than in the previous exercise, and it is a powerful tool if you have strong negative emotion that have been lingering in you. Do the following:

1. Sit down and make yourself comfortable.
2. Close your eyes and allow yourself to relax.
3. Place your attention on your breath as it enters and exits your body, focusing on the sensations you experience as you inhale and exhale.
4. If you are not already experiencing a negative emotion, relive a memory that will activate one. Think of a negative experience from the past or that you are currently experiencing.
5. When the negative emotion appears, identity what the emotion **feels** like. Notice: You want to describe what the emotion feels like, not what you think about it. In order to avoid falling in this trap, phrase your response as "It feels like_____?

Here are some examples:

- "It feels like it is crushing me."
- "I feel like I want to run away."

- "It leaves me feeling numb."
- "It feels like a boulder crushing me."

6. After you identify what the emotion feels like, repeat this process with the response that you give. Example:

    a. If the emotion that I am feeling is anger, my response to what it feels like is "It feels like my body is tightening."
    b. I would then repeat the process by asking "What does the tightening of the body feel like?
    c. My response to that could be "It feels like my body is hard."
    d. I would follow up with "What does a hard body feel like?"
    e. With every response that I give, I would repeat the same line of questioning until the emotion transforms into a positive emotion.

When trying to identify the feeling of an emotion, go by the first answer that comes to you. Do not worry about getting it wrong; you can't. As long as you describe the feeling of the emotion without getting intellectual about it, you will be on the right track. Every time you describe an emotion, you allow it to transform itself. By continuously describing it every time that it transforms, the emotion will eventually transform into a positive emotion.

Using this process facilitates the emotion to go full circle and heal itself.

If you feel that you were successful with the previous exercises, you are ready for next exercise, which involves meditation. Rather than concentrating awareness, meditation is for expanding awareness by not focusing on anything particular; rather, it involves observing all of experience.

Exercise 6

1. Sit down and allow yourself to relax.
2. Breathing naturally, place your attention on the flow of your breath as you inhale and exhale, noticing the sensations that you experience.
3. As you continue to observe your breath, you will experience a rhythm kick in where you become aware of your breathing without directing your awareness toward it. When this happens, move to step 4.
4. Without focusing your attention on anything, allow yourself to become an observer of all your experiences. Thoughts, sensations, perceptions, emotions, and sounds will all arise within you. Do not interpret, judge, identify, or analyzing anything that you experience. Simply remain as the one that is observing.

5. As you are aware of thoughts, sensations, emotions, and perceptions, realize that they are not you. You are aware of them, but they cannot be you.
6. Our thoughts encompass the entirety of that which we identify with. Your past, your anticipation of the future, your dreams, your knowledge, your past experiences, time, space, action, identification, your body, your mind, your sense of self, they are all conceptual thoughts from which you constructed your sense of self. But how can thoughts be you when you are the one that is aware of them?
7. During this meditation, you may have had thoughts like "Am I doing this right?" "This is too hard," "This is boring," and so on. While doing this exercise, get rid of all your expectations of what should be happening or what you should be experiencing. Everything that passes through your awareness is just an aspect of your consciousness. Acknowledge it with your awareness of it and then let it go. Do not hang-on, seek, or pursue anything.
8. Anything that you are aware of cannot be who you are. You cannot be something and be aware of it at the same time.
9. Who are you? Search for the existence of that which you refer to as "you." Can you find it?
10. Know this, anything that you believe to be you cannot be you. It cannot be you because you are aware of it.

If you are unable to find that which you refer to you as "you," do not feel frustrated; your failure to find "you" is actually a sign of success. Anything that can perceived, discerned, felt, or heard, measured, has color, or has size is considered phenomenal. The phenomenal world is the only world that our minds know. As awareness, you are non-phenomenal, meaning that you cannot be known by your five senses or your mind. Anything that you can know is not you; the truth of who you are cannot not be known. You are like the light of the sun as the light of the sun is invisible until its different wave lengths are broken down as experienced through a prism or rainbow.

If you are not your thoughts or experiences, how can you have a problem? How can you grow old or ill? What is there to do? What is it that you need? What is it that you need to complete when you identify yourself as the awareness of your experience? As awareness, how can you be separate from anything? From the perspective of awareness, what is there to fear or hope for?

This exercise is by far the most difficult exercise; however, it is only difficult because of how our minds have been conditioned to believe that we are a mind and body that is separate from the rest of life. This last exercise was a direct challenge to all your conceptual thinking that has been ingrained in you since the day you were born. If you truly want to live a life of profound happiness and freedom, continue to practice all the exercises until you feel comfortable with them, and you experience the realizations that have been described.

Though you are encouraged to practice these exercises, do not fall into the trap of "trying," "achieving" "making effort," "not getting it" or "getting it." All of these conceptual thoughts of the mind are the very things that you do not want to engage in. All of these thoughts will come; just do not give them the power of your attention. All of these exercises are intended to guide you toward recognizing your illusionary sense of self and gaining greater awareness of your true self, which is emptiness.

More on Buddhist philosophy

In the previous chapters, you were introduced to a number of exercises whereby you could develop greater control of your mind and challenge how you experience yourself and reality. In this chapter, we will discuss some specific Buddhist principles so as to provide greater context for your understanding.

The search for the self

In the previous exercises, you were offered guidance to the truth of yourself. The vast majority of people believe that they are a separate and distinct entity. They define themselves by their thoughts, their memories, and experiences as well as their physical bodies and their appearances. Because of this, we see ourselves as unique individuals who are separate from other living and nonliving beings.

The Buddhist principle of non-substantiality states that nothing in life exist as a separate entity unto itself; rather, everything that exists is a culmination of all that exists. To better elucidate this, let us use the example of a flower. With our conceptual minds, we see a flower as a separate entity from everything else. We do not confuse a flower with a rain drop, a cloud, a ray of sun light, the soil, the gardener who tends the flower, or a farm. We see each of these as separate entities. Further, if we were asked what a flower is made of, we may mention its petals, its stem, its leave, and its roots.

From a Buddhist perspective, a flower is made of what we can refer to as "non-flower parts." Without rain, the flower could not exist. Rain comes from clouds, so without clouds, the flower cannot exist. The flower depends on sunlight for photosynthesis, so the existence of the flower is dependent on the sun. The soil, which contains nutrients and holds the water for the flower, is also vital for the existence of the flower. The flower is also dependent on the gardener who tends it and looks after its needs, making it also a vital part of the flower's existence. Because the gardener needs to eat, the farm becomes indirectly vital for the flower's existence. The rain drop, the cloud, the sun, the soil, the gardener, and the farm can be referred to non-flower parts. Further, every non-flower part is void of a separate self. The rain is made of "non-rain parts," as are all the other non-flower parts just described. At the most essential level of the universe, the true entity of the flower is the entire universe. If just one "non-flower part" failed to exist, then the flower could not exist. From this perspective, the flower contains the entire universe, while providing evidence for the existence of the universe itself.

Going back to the last meditation, everything that you will ever experience is part of your "non-you" self. The aspect of you that is the awareness of all experience is your true self. Since there is only one consciousness, your true self is the same true self of all living beings that have ever existed or will exist.

If you truly understand this principle in your heart, instead of intellectually, you will experience a level of joy and connection with life that is most rare. Study this principle with your heart, and you will never again take life or yourself too seriously.

The Four Noble Truths

The Four Noble Truths are foundational Buddhist principles from which many Buddhist teachings are based on. The Four Noble Truths are as follows:

The first Noble Truth concerns suffering and is referred to as Dukkha. Dukkha is the term used for all sufferings, from the very mild to the most severe. Suffering is an inescapable aspect of living in this world, this is the first Noble Truth.

The second Noble Truth is that Dukkha is causal in its appearance in this world. The cause of Dukkha comes from our tendency toward attachments or aversion. Anytime we try to control life by grasping or clinging to the physical world, it will lead to suffering. Similarly, when we hold an aversion toward anything in life, this too will lead to suffering. Suffering arises because we identify with that which we are attached to or are avoiding. Further, suffering is based on the impermanence of life. All expressions of life are transitory, nothing is permanent.

The third Noble Truth is cessation of Dukkha, which is called Nirvana. Nirvana arises when we no longer identify with the world of form, including our bodies and thoughts. Nirvana can also be referred to as the world of Buddhahood.

The Fourth Noble Truth is also referred to as the Eight Fold Path; they are the paths that lead to Awakening:

The first path is that of correct view or understanding, meaning that we are able to perceive the illusions of the mind. The Sanskrit word for this path is Samma-Ditthi.

The second path is the path of correct thought. Correct thought comes from viewing the world through love and compassion. This path is known as Samma-Sankappa. Love and compassion arises when we are able to understand our own suffering and are not ruled by our attachments.

The third path is the path of correct speech. Correct speech is that which is compassionate, heartfelt, inspiring, and understood by the listener.

The fourth path is the path of correct action. Correct action is action that creates value for all stakeholders; it is ethical, and upholds our sense of dignity. This path is referred to as Samma-Kammanta.

The fifth path is the path of correct livelihood. This means that how we generate an income for ourselves is ethical and does not lead to exploitation of others. This is known as Samma-Ajiva.

The sixth path is the path of correct effort or energy. This can be understood as focus and diligence. Correct effort involves focusing our life force for the purpose of transforming our current experience in a manner that creates value or benefit for others and ourselves. When practicing correct effort, we become conscious creators who are taking action that is in alignment with all of life. The sixth path is known as Samma-Vayama.

The Seventh Noble Path is that of mindfulness. Mindfulness is an expanded awareness to all levels of experience. It means having awareness of our environment, other people, our thoughts, feelings, perceptions, and the nature of reality itself. This awareness is not a conceptual understanding; it is a deeper knowing that comes when we can experience our world in a way that is free of the illusions created by our minds. The Seventh Noble Path is known as "Samma-Sati."

The Eighth Noble Path is difficult to describe in words but it involves becoming fully integrated, becoming one, with our experience. It involves meditating so deeply that all sense of distinction or separateness fades and we become one with all. This is the meaning of Buddhahood or enlightenment. This final path is known as Samma-Samadhi.

Exercise 7

Review the section on the Four Noble Truths, remembering that they point to suffering that is caused by incorrect understanding of reality. This incorrect understanding of reality includes the illusions of the mind, attachment, incorrect speech, incorrect action, incorrect livelihood, incorrect effort or expenditure of energy, and a lack of mindfulness.

We can simplify this by reducing these down to one word, "Love." I want you to make it a daily goal to come from the point of love in how you perceive, how you think, how you speak, how you act, how you work, and how you expend effort. The following are examples on how to do this:

Perception and the illusions of our mind: We fall for the illusions of our mind, for our thoughts, because we believe them to be true. Given that many of thoughts create a sense of fear or concern in us, fear is what is brought into existence, it shows up in our experience.

Turn the tables on your mind and see yourself as the parent and your thoughts and emotions are your children. When you experience thoughts and emotions that create fear in you, view them with a sense of love and appreciation. Do not challenge your thoughts or emotions, do not try to change them, just accept them for what they are and observe them with a sense of love and caring. You can speak them just as you would speak to a frighten child.

Speaking: Whenever you speak to others or yourself, come from the perspective of love. This means that you do not judge, criticize, or devalue them in any way. Allow your speech to communicate compassion, honesty, and encouragement. Speak to others and yourself in a way that acknowledges the nobility of others and yourself. The truth of who we are is much greater than what is currently being experienced.

Actions: See your actions not as means to an end but rather a way to express your highest truth. Anybody can take action on a task. Become greater than your past by infusing your actions with a sense of love and compassion for all those who are affected by it.

Livelihood: Demonstrating love through your livelihood can take a variety of forms. It could mean finding a new way to support yourself that is more aligned with your values or it could be performing your current job in a way that causes you to focus on creating value for your employer, for your co-workers, and your customers. When this becomes your focus, you will transcend your job by making your work and expression of your love.

Expenditure of effort and energy: On a daily basis, are you largely directing your effort and energy toward activities in order to meet the expectations of others or out of a sense of obligation?

Or do you direct your energy toward activities that are meaningful for you, that are fulfilling, or out of a desire to create happiness for others and yourself. This has less to do with the nature of the activity than it does the meaning that the activity has for you and the value it creates for others.

Make it a goal that you will reserve as much of your efforts and energy for those things that bring you fulfilment. Nature is a master in energy efficiency as all actions that are displayed in the natural world lead to birth and growth, even in death.

When we allow our minds to direct us, much of our energy is spent on engaging in activities out of a sense of fear, guilt, or distracting ourselves form our thoughts and emotions.

You can select one of these five categories to practice each day of the week, or you can select one category to practice for the whole week. When you practice, commit to taking 3-5 minutes to devote to your selected category. As you become more skillful, you can extend this time frame. With continued practice, mindfulness will spontaneously arise within you.

The Buddhist perspective of God

Buddhism does not believe in a god that is separate from ourselves or outside of ourselves. Many religions, such as Christianity, view God as an omnipotent power that oversees our lives, passes judgments on us and is in charge of our lives.

In general, most Buddhist sects believe in what is best described as an ultimate reality. This ultimate reality is the source from which everything arises from, while at the same time it is found within all things. We and this ultimate reality are not separate from each other; in fact, we are it. Our lives and ultimate reality are one.

This ultimate reality does not pass judgment; it does not seek our devotion or belief in it. Judgment, punishment, reward, heaven or hell, good or bad, right or wrong, and devotion or disbelief is all created in the mind. When we can understand our minds, we can understand ourselves. When we understand ourselves, we become enlightened. Enlightenment has always existed within us, and it always will. The purpose of Buddhism is to get us to realize this for ourselves through direct experience.

Exercise 8

For many of us, our beliefs about God are cultivated through our upbringing and are never challenged or explored by us. One of the most primary questions we can ask ourselves about our beliefs or disbeliefs of God is simply that, "Is my beliefs about God just that, a belief?" A belief is simply a thought that we give a lot of attention to; our attention to a thought makes it true for us.

We can only experience that which the conceptual mind understands, meaning that we if we cannot detect something, we cannot have an experience of it. What about our sense of self, of that which we call "I," can this be detected? Have you heard, touched, or saw "I,"? Where is this "I" located? Is it located in the body? Is it located in the heart or mind? Regardless of how you answer these questions, you would then have to ask "Who or what knows this?" Who is it that is aware of the answers that you give? Who is aware of you? Again, regardless of how you answer this question, there must be something that is aware of it. How can we claim to know God without first understanding the true nature of who we are? Here are some practical steps you can take to explore these questions for yourself:

1. Regardless of what you believe about God or yourself, take time daily to become quiet and still. You can meditate or simply find a relaxing place to sit and become still within,

do not judge, evaluate, analyze, or think about anything, just observe.
2. Observe your thoughts, your sensations, your emotions, your feelings, the people around you, or your environment. Do not put any effort in your observation; just allow your attention to roam freely.
3. The only thing you need to do is observe, allow whatever happens to happen on its own accord. By practicing this exercise, you will learn to observe more deeply as you will have reduced the influence of the mind. With that will come a clearer understanding to the nature of God and you.

Living the Buddhist Teaching

After reading the previous chapters in this book, you may find Buddhism interesting but believe that its teachings are too difficult to understand or practice, that it would require a lot of work, or you may be concerned that practicing these teachings may conflict with your religious beliefs. My hope is that if you find Buddhism interesting that you will not let any of these concerns discourage you. First of all, though Buddhism is recognized as a religion that was not originally its intent.

Buddhism is more of a science of the mind. It views the world in a practical and realistic manner that is testable; it does not require faith; more important than faith is your actual experience when practicing its teachings. If you find that its teachings enrich your life, then faith will follow. Further, its teachings are applicable to any religious or spiritual tradition that you may belong to, even science is reaching conclusions that mirror Buddhist thought. For this reason, you do not have to give-up your religious beliefs; you do not even have to consider yourself Buddhist. This book is in no way intended to teach you how to become a Buddhist. If this is your desire, I recommend you contact a Buddhist community within your neighborhood.

Bonus Chapter: The Skills of Mindfulness

1. **Observe.** Watch your thought pattern as you drift and respond to things around you. No judging, no assuming. Just watching.

Specifically with your emotions:

- Notice the experience of your emotion
- Notice your emotions without getting caught in your emotions. Don't try to add anything in – or take anything out.
- Say to yourself: "I notice that I am feeling joy/sorrow/fear/anxiety."
- Just see what flows past your awareness.
- Be alert as you observe what flows to, round and through you.
- Notice what comes through your senses, all that you smell, touch, hear, say, feel, and taste.

2. **Describe.** Put words in the experience. When a thought or a feeling arises, put words on it, acknowledge it. Don't be worried if this seems strange and unnatural at first. If your emotional role models have taught you to ignore or belittle your emotions, you may be very well practised at being the opposite of attentive and mindful of your own experience.

You can also try some of the following statements for practice. Over time you will find your own voice. Say in your mind: "A thought 'this is too much for me' has just come to my mind." When you are nervous say, "My stomach muscles are tightening." Describe what is happening, keep it factual as you talk to yourself, call a thought a thought, and call an emotion an emotion. Stay descriptive and keep everything simple.

3. **Participate.** As a practice to repeat over and over, mindfulness helps you be an active part of your own life. Fully enter your experience, but without loving or hating it. Be as fully involved in each moment as you can be, participating in each moment as it comes, one moment, then another, staying in the *now* if the moment calls for you to be here now. Let yourself worry fully, let go of it fully, observe fully, describe fully - enjoy the process.

Be your experience, completely forgetting yourself. Drift away from the idea of worrying about how other people see you or whether you are doing as well as someone else. Don't focus on concerns about perfection or pleasing other people. Give your full attention to the experience here and now. Think of Olympic athletes, who seem so absorbed with their sport or performance, appearing unaware that the world is watching them. They give themselves fully to what they are doing at that moment, they are in their experience.

Here are a few examples of ways to develop and articulate mindfulness. You will soon develop your own, of course.

When You Feel Happy

- ☐ "I notice that I am laughing...I observe that I feel energized."
- ☐ "I notice a sensation of strength...I observe that I feel centered."

When You Feel Anxiety

- ☐ "I observe that I am experiencing anxiety...I notice the urge to avoid the person I disappointed."
- ☐ "I observe the thought that 'I am useless at everything'...I notice the desire to beat myself up."

Activity

Now that you have read over these examples put this book down, sit upright, close your eyes, (after you have done reading these instructions), and take one gentle breath. Observe your current emotions and sensations. What do you notice? Describe what you notice, avoiding judgments about the goodness or badness of what you feel or think. Stay descriptive.

BONUS EXCERCISES:

We will start off this chapter with a meditation whose purpose is to bring you to a greater level awareness as to the nature of who you are. Do the following:

1. Find a comfortable place to sit, and close your eyes. Try to keep your back as straight as possible while remaining relaxed and comfortable.
2. As in the previous exercises, focus on the sensations of your breath, making sure that you are breathing normally.
3. It is important that while you are doing this meditation that you put absolutely no effort into what you doing. For most us, we are so conditioned to try to achieve a certain result, or we have expectations of what we should be experiencing. When this happens, we either start doubting ourselves or become frustrated. I want you to completely accept whatever arises in your experience, don't try to change anything. There is no such thing as getting it right or wrong.
4. As you observe your breathe, you will experience thoughts, sensations, feelings, and sounds. Let them come and go on their own accord.

5. Anytime your mind wanders, gently return it to your breathing.

6. As you continue to focus on your breath, you will notice your mind will become more still, more quiet. It is important to note that before reaching this calm, you will most likely experience a burst of activity in your mind. Do not get distracted by this as it is natural. If and when this happens, just continue to focus on your breath until your mind calms down.

7. As your continue observing your breath, you will notice that it will take less of our attention to observe it; you will not have to remind yourself to focus on it. This is an indication that you have gone to a deeper level of awareness.

8. Relax your attention and simply observe whatever comes into your awareness. Notice how thought, sensation, emotions, and feelings arise from the depths of your awareness and then fade away. Nothing that you can experience is permanent; all phenomena are transient and in constant flux. Thoughts appear and the fade away. Sensations and emotions change in their level of intensity.

Even if you here a sound that is continuous, it will fluctuate in its intensity.

9. Allow yourself to experience everything that comes into the light of your awareness; offer complete acceptance to all of your experiences. Do not at any point of this mediation use your imagination or create a meaning for your experience. Let all of your experiences come and go on their own accord.

10. Notice that you are aware of thought but that you are not thought. You are aware of sensation but that you are not sensation. You experience feelings but you are not feelings. When you have a troubling thought, awareness is not troubled. You may be feeling peaceful, but awareness is neither peaceful nor disturbed. You are aware of all experience yet awareness is untouched by all of experience.

11. Who is the one that is aware of experience? Can you reveal the identity of the one that is aware? Search for the one that is aware. Who is this one? You may say "I am the one that is aware," or "consciousness is aware," or "my higher power is aware." To say any of these things requires awareness of them as well. How can these be the source of awareness when awareness is required to know of their

existence? In fact, regardless of how you answer this question, there must be awareness of it. Thoughts of "I", "me," "spirit," "soul," or "higher power," are simply that, thoughts. Keep searching, do not give up. Try to find the one that is the source of awareness.

Final Thoughts

This book offered numerous perspectives on how you can live a happier and more peaceful life. Because Buddhist philosophy is so drastically different from conventional thinking, many of you may find the contents of this book difficult to understand. What is important to keep in mind is that Buddhism, as with any philosophy or way of thinking is not the inherent answer to finding that which you desire for your life. All teachings, regardless of their teacher or the faith that they belong to, are nothing more than sign posts that are pointing to us the direction. To believe, as many people do, that the teaching itself is the answer is to say that the road sign for the Holiday Inn is the hotel itself. There is a story of a body who wanted to learn about Buddhism. He had heard that there was a very wise Buddhist monk that lived in a small hut not far from his village. The boy finds the monk who is out in his field looking at the moon. The monk called his dog, who came running to him enthusiastically. The monk pointed his finger at the moon, but the dog focus only on his finger. The monk then told the body, "Do not confuse the finger for the moon." In the same manner, do not let these Buddhist teachings confuse you from what you are looking for. Instead, treat them like a guide who is giving a tour of a museum or a hiking trail; the experience you have is dependent on you, not the guide.

Conclusion

If you enjoyed this book and found something to experiment with, try out, share or commit to we are delighted.

Health and happiness can be found through many avenues and for all of them the journey itself is usually the joy. The destination is what we want to achieve, but it is in getting there that we constantly find out more about ourselves and our own uniqueness. And this is the most fascinating of all.

Until we meet again in another book – be healthy, be happy, be beautiful inside and out.

Sending you lots of love from here,

Maya Faro

For similar books and audiobooks, visit:

www.YourWellnessBooks.com

www.LOAforSuccess.com

More Books Written by Maya Faro

Available in Your Local Amazon Store

-kindle-audio-paperback-

(just search for "Maya Faro")

www.ingramcontent.com/pod-product-compliance
Lightning Source LLC
Chambersburg PA
CBHW071031080526
44587CB00015B/2573